Moving

By Meg Gaertner

www.littlebluehousebooks.com

Little Blue House is distributed by North Star Editions:
sales@northstareditions.com | 888-417-0195

Produced for Little Blue House by Red Line Editorial.

Photographs ©: Shutterstock Images, cover, 4, 7, 8 (top), 8 (bottom), 13, 14, 17, 19 (top), 19 (bottom), 21, 24 (bottom right); iStockphoto, 11, 23, 24 (top left), 24 (top right), 24 (bottom left)

Library of Congress Control Number: 2021916804

ISBN
978-1-64619-487-2 (hardcover)
978-1-64619-514-5 (paperback)
978-1-64619-566-4 (ebook pdf)
978-1-64619-541-1 (hosted ebook)

Printed in the United States of America
Mankato, MN
012022

About the Author

Meg Gaertner enjoys reading, writing, dancing, and being outside. She lives in Minnesota.

Table of Contents

Moving

People move for many reasons.

A parent might get a job in a new city.

A growing family might need a bigger home.

Or a family might get a smaller home to save money.

family

Mixed Feelings

Maybe you're feeling hopeful about moving somewhere new.

Or maybe you're mad that the move is happening.

Maybe you're sad about leaving your friends.
Or maybe you're scared about making new ones.

Maybe you feel many things
at once.
It's okay to feel all of
these things.
Moving is a big change.

Feeling Better

Let your family know how you feel.

Ask questions about the new home.

Ask about the new school and neighborhood, too.

Maybe you can even visit the new place.

Put your favorite things in one box.

At your new home, you can unpack that box first.

Then you will have the things you need to feel at home.

box

You might miss your old home and friends.

Take lots of pictures to put in your new bedroom.

The pictures will help you remember.

picture

Get your friends' phone numbers and addresses.

That way, you can call your friends to talk.

You can also send them letters.

You might even be able to go back and visit them.

letter

It may take time to get used to the new place.

But you will make it your own.

Soon, you will feel at home there.

Glossary

friends

neighborhood

letters

pictures

Index